Learning Short-take

MAKING MEETINGS WORK

Getting the most out of meetings

CATHERINE MATTISKE

TPC - The Performance Company Pty Ltd
Level 20, Darling Park
Tower 2, 201 Sussex Street,
Sydney NSW 2000
Australia

ACN 077 455 273
email: tpc@tpc.net.au
Website: www.catherinemattiske.com

© TPC – The Performance Company Pty Limited
First edition published in 2006
Second edition published in 2011
Third edition published in 2022

All rights reserved. Apart from any fair dealing for the purposes of study, research or review, as permitted under Australian copyright law, no part of this publication may be reproduced by any means without the written permission of the copyright owner. Every effort has been made to obtain permission relating to information reproduced in this publication.

The information in this publication is based on the current state of commercial and industry practice, applicable legislation, general law and the general circumstances as at the date of publication. No person shall rely on any of the contents of this publication and the publisher and the author expressly exclude all liability for direct and indirect loss suffered by any person resulting in any way from the use of or reliance on this publication or any part of it. Any options and advice are offered solely in pursuance of the author's and the publisher's intention to provide information, and have not been specifically sought.

For eBook version: By payment of the required fees, you have been granted the non-exclusive, non-transferable right to access and read the text of this e-book on screen. No part of this text may be reproduced, transmitted, downloaded, decompiled, reverse engineered, or stored in or introduced into any information storage retrieval system, in any form or by any means, whether the electronic or mechanical, now known or hereinafter invented, without the express permission of the author.

 A catalogue record for this book is available from the National Library of Australia

National Library of Australia
Cataloguing-in-Publication data

Mattiske, Catherine
Making Meetings Work: Getting the Most out of Meetings

ISBN 978-1-921547-14-0

1. Occupational training 2. Learning I. Title

370.113

Distributed by TPC - The Performance Company - www.catherinemattiske.com
For further information contact TPC - The Performance Company, Sydney Australia on +61 (02) 9555 1953.

HELLO.

Welcome to the Learning Short-take® process!

This Learning Short-take® is a bite sized learning package that aims to improve your skills and provide you with an opportunity for personal and professional development to achieve success in your role.

This Learning Short-take® combines self study with workplace activities in a unique learning system to keep you motivated and energized. So let's get started!

Step 1:
What's inside?

- Learning Short-take®. This section contains all of the learning content and will guide you through the learning process.
- Learning Activities. You will be prompted to complete these as you read through.
- Learning Journal. This is a summary of your key learnings. Update it when prompted.
- Skill Development Action Plan. Learning is about taking action. This is your action plan where you'll plan how you will implement your learning.

Step 2:
Complete the Learning Short-take®

- Learning Short-takes® are best completed in a quiet environment that is free of distractions.
- Schedule time in your calendar to complete the Learning Short-take® and prioritize this time as an investment in your own professional development.
- Depending on the title, most participants complete the Learning Short-take® from 90 minutes to 2.5 hours.

Step 3:
Meet with your Manager/Coach

- Schedule a 30 minute meeting with your Manager or Coach.
- At this meeting share your completed Activities, Learning Journal and Skill Development Action Plan.
- Most importantly, discuss and agree on how you will implement your learning in your role.

GET VIP ACCESS TO YOUR MATERIALS

This Learning Short-take® includes an interactive activity book, associated tools and job aids, plus a bonus eBook.

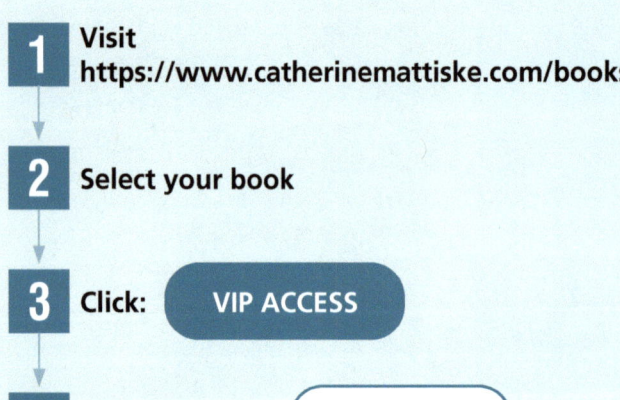

1 Visit https://www.catherinemattiske.com/books

2 Select your book

3 Click: **VIP ACCESS**

4 Enter the code: MMW2022245

WELCOME

Making Meetings Work
Getting the Most out of Meetings

Making Meetings Work combines self-study with realistic workplace activities to provide you with the key skills and techniques to make meetings work. Your meetings will become more focused, efficient, targeted and more likely to have a productive impact on the company's bottom-line. You will learn how to more effectively prepare, manage, facilitate and actively participate in meetings.

It is estimated that the average professional spends 21.5 hours per month in meetings, or approximately two weeks every year. It is also estimated that at least 50% of this time is wasted in unproductive meeting activity. **Making Meetings Work** will provide you with the tools to help you save time and money.

Making Meetings Work includes the **Meeting Administration Checklist, Meeting Agenda** and **Meeting Minutes** provided as free downloadable tools.

Now let's get started!

1	Learning Short-take® Start here
2	Learning Journal 73
3	Skill Development Action Plan 79
4	Quick Reference 85
5	Next Steps 97

"Effective meetings don't happen by accident, they happen by design."

"*The most important thing in communication is to hear what isn't being said.*"

PETER F. DRUCKER

Section 1
LEARNING SHORT-TAKE®

WHAT'S IN THIS LEARNING SHORT-TAKE®

Table of Contents

How to Complete Your Learning Short-take®	5
Activity Checklist	6
Learning Objectives	7
Let's Get Started	8
Part 1 - The Business of Meetings	9
The Business of Meetings	10
Strategies for Fixing Unproductive Meetings	19
Part 2 - Meeting Types	25
Types of Meetings	26
Meeting Purpose	29
Part 3 - Meeting Process	31
The Meeting Process	32
Step 1 - Plan the Meeting	32
Step 2 - Prepare the Agenda	38
Step 3 - Conduct the Meeting	45
Part 4 - Bringing Meetings to Life	63
Making Meetings more Lively	64
International Meeting Etiquette	68
Part 5 - In Summary	71
In Summary - Making Meetings Work	72

© 2022, TPC - The Performance Company Pty Limited. All rights reserved.

HOW TO COMPLETE YOUR LEARNING SHORT-TAKE®

1. **Reflect on your skills and abilities** in preparing for and conducting meetings, and how you use this information to improve effectiveness in your role.

2. **Complete the Activities** as directed.

3. Highlight specific skill areas that you believe you could develop more. Add these to the **Learning Journal**. Add to your Learning Journal as you go.

4. When you have completed this Learning Short-take® **meet with your Manager/Coach**. In this meeting, you will jointly establish a personal **Skill Development Action Plan**.

5. **Subject to your coach's final review** and assessment, you will either sign off the module, or undertake further skill development as appropriate.

ACTIVITY CHECKLIST

During this Learning Short-take® you will be prompted to complete the following activities:

- Activity 1 - Meeting Evaluation — 15
- Activity 2 - Personal Assessment — 16
- Activity 3 - The Cost of Meetings — 18
- Activity 4 - Meeting Strategies — 24
- Activity 5 - What Type of Meeting Am I? — 27
- Activity 6 - Meeting Planner — 34
- Activity 7 - Worksheet for Next 6 Meetings — 37
- Activity 8 - Meeting Agenda — 41
- Activity 9 - Meeting Administration Checklist — 42
- Activity 10 - Meeting Minutes — 47
- Activity 11 - Handling Difficult Meeting Situations — 60
- Learning Journal — 73
- Skill Development Action Plan — 79

LEARNING OBJECTIVES

By the end of this Learning Short-take® participants should be able to:

- Evaluate your current level of meeting success.
- Identify the various types of meetings and explain key differences.
- Develop solutions to common meeting problems.
- Outline the steps for a successful meeting.
- Carry out meeting planning and preparation.
- Create a Skill Development Action Plan.

"If you wouldn't write it and sign it, don't say it."

EARL WILSON

LET'S GET STARTED

Recent workplace productivity studies, reported by Truelist, Apollo Technical, Atlassian and Finances Online, show that on average workers attend 62 meetings per month. In one month, up to 31 hours can be spent in unproductive meetings. Up to 68% of workers have lost time due to disorganized, poorly planned meetings. 40% of workers experience significant distractions from colleagues dropping in for a spontaneous meeting.

The sharp rise in remote working, global teams operating virtually, and the paradigm of virtual fatigue give rise to greater challenges for maintaining attention and engagement during meetings. Productivity statistics demonstrate an overwhelming lack of engagement and effectiveness:

- 96% of workers have missed meetings
- 91% of workers daydream or 'drift off' in a meeting
- 89% complain about disorganized, ineffective meetings
- 73% tend to 'multi-task' and do other work
- 50% of workers consider meetings a waste of time
- 45% feel an overload of too many meetings
- 39% admit to falling asleep in meetings!

Meetings, therefore consume a large percentage of our working week, yet can significantly improve in productivity. This is a poor return on investment for organizations and is well below what would be considered acceptable for other investments. Regardless of whether you are meeting in-person, via phone, virtually, or holding a hybrid meeting, advanced meeting skills are imperative in today's fast-paced business environment.

This Learning Short-take® combines self-study with workplace activities to provide you with the key skills and techniques to make meetings work. Your meetings will become focused, efficient, targeted, and more likely to have a productive impact on the company's bottom-line. You will learn how to effectively prepare, manage, facilitate and actively participate in meetings. The Learning Short-take® is designed for completion in approximately 90 minutes.

THE BUSINESS OF MEETINGS

PART 1

THE BUSINESS OF MEETINGS

Meetings dominate the way in which we do business today. In fact, millions of meetings occur in the U.S. each day, and since February 2020 the average number of weekly meetings taking place has increased by 153%[1]. Although many of us complain about meetings, we can all expect to spend our work time immersed in them.

Why Do Meetings Fail?

Meetings can fail for one or more of the following reasons:

1. **The meeting is unnecessary** - communication of information, or call to action could have been achieved via alternate means.
2. **The meeting is held for the wrong reason** - the agenda does not include issues of real importance.
3. **The objective of the meeting is unclear** - there is no identified aim or outcome of the meeting.
4. **The wrong people are present** - real decision makers are absent.
5. **The agenda is not properly controlled** - action items are not given the right amount of time, attention or structure. There is no real meeting process in place.
6. **It takes place in a disagreeable environment** - the environment is not conducive to reaching consent on important issues.
7. **The meeting is poorly timed** - attendees have other pressing commitments and/or the meeting has been scheduled at an inconvenient time.
8. **The process is subject to poor decision making** - the meeting has not been structured to enable decisions to be made and responsibilities assigned.

---

[1] Microsoft 2022 Work Trend Index: Annual Report. March 16, 2022.

The Impact of Unproductive Meetings

Direct effects of unproductive meetings include:
- Meetings are longer, less efficient and generate fewer results.
- More meetings are needed to accomplish objectives.
- With so much time spent in ineffective meetings, employees have less time to get their own work done.
- Ineffective meetings create frustration for all attendees.
- Information generated in unproductive meetings usually isn't managed properly.
- Inefficient meetings cost organizations billions of dollars each year in otherwise productive employee work time.

Although there is a general consensus among professionals today that meetings could be more productive, very few seem willing to make a commitment to improve them. There are a number of reasons for 'meeting complacency':

- Most individuals have never experienced or witnessed the power of a truly effective meeting and, therefore, don't recognize the importance of having better meetings.
- For many, it may seem more "convenient" to continue current meeting practices, regardless of how inefficient they may be.
- Many teams don't have access to the kind of effective meeting information they need to improve their meetings.
- Most employees feel there's hardly enough time in a day to complete basic tasks. Who has the time or energy to commit to improving meetings?
- Managers, in general, fail to consider the negative impact meetings have on the organization's bottom line.

"We have the most ineffective meetings of any company I've ever seen."

To Meet or Not to Meet?

Deciding to hold a meeting should be a serious business consideration.

12 reasons people need to meet:

1. To communicate or request vital information.
2. When you need a group consensus.
3. To respond to questions or concerns.
4. When you need a decision or an evaluation on an issue.
5. When you need acceptance or support of an idea.
6. To sell an idea, product or service.
7. To brainstorm ideas.
8. To solve a problem, conflict or difference of opinion.
9. To generate a sense of team spirit.
10. To provide training or clarification of a project.
11. To provide reassurance on an issue or situation.
12. To create an awareness or interest in an idea, situation or project.

12 Reasons *Not* to Hold a Meeting:

1. When you meet for the sake of meeting - same time, same place, every week.
2. When someone's ego gets in the way and they want to look important and in control.
3. When the information could be better communicated another way.
4. When key people are unavailable.
5. When participants don't have time to prepare.
6. When your decision is made and you don't want any input.
7. When the costs are greater than the benefits.
8. When other issues blur the decision at hand.
9. When the subject matter is confidential.
10. When nothing would be gained or lost by not having a meeting.
11. When you have nothing else to do and want to look busy.
12. When you want an excuse to get out of the office.

"Meetings are a symptom of bad organization. The fewer meetings the better."

PETER F. DRUCKER

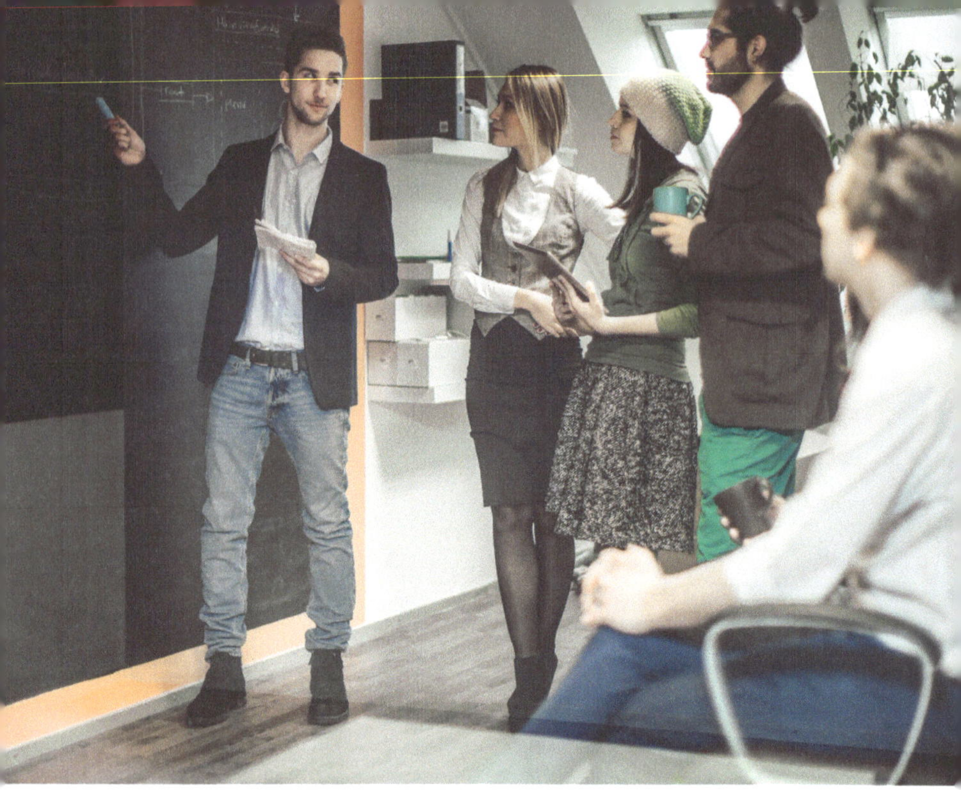

Complete Activity # 1
Meeting Evaluation

Complete Activity # 2
Personal Assessment

Complete Activity # 3
The Cost of Meetings

ACTIVITY 1: MEETING EVALUATION

Consider the typical meeting you attend in business. Compare your meeting to the following characteristics of an effective meeting. Place a check mark (✔) next to those statements that apply to meetings you normally conduct or attend.

		Always	Sometimes	Rarely
1.	An agenda is prepared prior to the meeting.			
2.	Meeting participants have an opportunity to contribute to the agenda.			
3.	Advance notice of meeting time and place is provided to those invited.			
4.	Meeting facilities are comfortable and adequate for the number of participants.			
5.	The meeting begins on time.			
6.	The meeting has a scheduled ending time.			
7.	The use of time is monitored throughout the meeting.			
8.	Everyone has an opportunity to present his or her point of view.			
9.	Participants listen attentively to each other.			
10.	There are periodic summaries as the meeting progresses.			
11.	No one tends to dominate the discussion.			
12.	Everyone has a voice in decisions made at the meeting.			
13.	The meeting typically ends with a summary of accomplishments.			
14.	The meeting is periodically evaluated by participants.			
15.	People can be depended upon to carry out any action agreed to during the meeting.			
16.	A memorandum of discussion or minutes of the meeting is provided to each participant following the meeting.			
17.	The meeting leader follows up with participants on action agreed to during the meeting.			
18.	The appropriate and necessary people can be counted on to attend each meeting.			
19.	The decision process used is appropriate for the size of the group.			
20.	When used, audiovisual equipment is in good working condition and does not detract from the meeting.			
	Total			

Now update your Learning Journal (page 73)

ACTIVITY 2: PERSONAL ASSESSMENT

Consider the typical meeting you lead and attend. Compare yourself to the following characteristics of an effective meeting leaders and attendees. Place a check mark (✔) next to those statements that apply to meetings you normally conduct or attend.

	Always	Sometimes	Rarely
As a Meeting Leader			
1. I have clear objectives for meetings.			
2. I am selective about who I invite to meetings.			
3. I prepare an agenda and distribute it with the meeting invitation.			
4. I ask attendees for their input to the agenda and update the agenda prior to the meeting.			
5. I arrive early for meetings that I lead.			
6. I start at the scheduled start time.			
7. I follow the agenda.			
8. I manage time and finish at the scheduled finish time.			
9. I encourage all attendees to participate.			
10. I ask questions to ensure all attendees have an opportunity to put forward their points of view.			
11. I handle any conflict or disagreement that may arise confidently and professionally.			
12. I facilitate discussion and keep the meeting on track.			
13. I summarize decisions.			
14. I distribute minutes of the meeting.			
15. I request feedback from attendees on the success of the meeting (either during the meeting or after the meeting).			
16. I follow up on action items with those who have been assigned tasks.			
Total			

ACTIVITY 2: CONTINUED

	Always	Sometimes	Rarely
As a Meeting Attendee			
1. I know the purpose of meetings I attend.			
2. I confirm my attendance to the meeting and once confirmed always attend.			
3. I prepare for the meeting (in line with the agenda).			
4. I arrive a few minutes early for the meeting.			
5. I contribute ideas to the discussion, ask questions where I am uncertain, and refrain from side conversations during the meeting.			
6. I listen intently to other attendees during the meeting.			
7. I am always focused on the meeting. That is, I never conduct other work during meetings (such as checking my phone, emails, writing notes on other issues or any other work that is not directly related to the meeting).			
8. I contribute professionally and without emotional outbursts.			
9. I provide feedback to the meeting leader on what went well and what could have gone better during the meeting.			
10. I follow-up on my assigned tasks in a timely manner.			
Total			

Now update your Learning Journal (page 73)

ACTIVITY 3: THE COST OF MEETINGS

A meeting should be well organized and have a primary goal. Getting together for a 'chat' or an 'update' does not work and is a waste of time - plus a waste of money.
How much do your meetings cost?
Reflect on either the last meeting you attended or your next meeting scheduled.
Calculate the approximate cost of the meeting.

	Sample	Calculate the approximate cost
Average salary per annum	$80,000	
Average hourly salary (annual salary divided by 48 weeks divided by 28 hours per week) (PPC study concluded average weekly working hours were 45. 17 of those hours were unproductive, resulting in only 28 productive hours per week)	$60	
Multiplied by number of people	Say 5 in the team $300 per hour	
Meeting duration (2 hours) = 10 people hours	$600 for 2 hour meeting + opportunity cost of having 10 hours of lost sales productivity + travel time + preparation time	
	What is the true cost of your meetings?	$
Venue Costs	Add any venue or virtual meeting software costs (room, catering, audio visual or technical equipment)	$
Total	Add True Cost + Venue Costs	$

Now update your Learning Journal (page 73)

STRATEGIES FOR FIXING UNPRODUCTIVE MEETINGS

In a business world that is faster, tougher and leaner than ever, you might expect the demands of competition to curb our appetite for meetings. In reality, the opposite may be true. As more work becomes teamwork, and fewer people remain to do the work that exists, the number of meetings is likely to increase rather than decrease.

Meetings are the most universal, and universally despised part of business life. But bad meetings do more than ruin an otherwise pleasant day. However, a variety of tools and techniques can make meetings less painful and more productive.

1. Adopt the mind-set that meetings are real work.

Too often, attendees don't take meetings seriously. They arrive late, leave early, and while in attendance, daydream or doodle. People don't view going to meetings as doing real work. That all-too-frequent expression of relief, "Meeting's over, let's get back to work" is the mortal enemy of good meetings. Disciplined meetings require a change in mind-set and a shared conviction among all participants that meetings are real work.

Ask the following questions for every meeting:

- Do you know the purpose of this meeting?
- Do you have an agenda?
- Do you know your role?
- Do you follow the rules for good minutes?

"We realize our meetings are unproductive. A consulting firm is trying to help us, and we think they've hit the mark. But we've got a long way to go."

2. Track the cost of your meetings and use technology to make them more productive.

Time is money and meetings are typically twice as long as they need to be. Where possible use modern technologies, platforms and delivery methods such as interactive whiteboards and digital collaboration software to make the best possible use of the meeting time available. Employing these technologies will allow meeting participants to access information instantly, share data and automatically save information generated during their meetings.

Alternatively, use email pre and post meeting to share information quickly and avert the need for follow-up meetings.

Videoconferencing and virtual meeting software are commonly used tools to communicate across distances, reducing the number of actual face-to-face meetings.

3. Get serious about agendas and minimize distractions.

Meeting attendees are prone to wander off the topic and can spend more time digressing than discussing. A good, solid agenda will avert this problem and communicate to attendees that the meeting should be taken seriously. Circulate the agenda several days before a meeting to let participants react to it and modify it if necessary. The agenda should list the meeting's key topics, who will lead the discussion, how long each topic will take, what the expected outcomes are, and so on.

"We just seem to meet and meet and meet and we never seem to do anything."

Of course, even the best-crafted agendas can't guard against digressions, distractions, and the other foibles of human interaction. The challenge is to keep meetings focused without stifling creativity or insulting participants who stray. When comments come up that aren't related to the issue at hand use a Parking Lot (a flipchart or digital whiteboard) to maintain the focus. Remember it's a Parking Lot, not a Black Hole! That means someone in the meeting needs to track and take responsibility for the Parking Lot issues.

4. Convert Decisions into Action

The problem isn't that people are lazy or irresponsible, it is merely that participants leave meetings with different views of what happened and what is supposed to happen next. Meeting experts are unanimous on this point: even with effective meeting tools for organizing and sharing ideas, ie. whiteboards, flip charts, Post-it™ notes etc, the capacity for misunderstanding is unlimited. The best way to avoid misunderstanding is to convert from "meeting" to "doing", where the "doing" focuses on the creation of shared documents or using virtual collaboration boards that lead to action. Using a laptop and projector or a virtual meeting platform with shared screen, the minute taker can record comments, outline ideas, and generate proposals, enabling the entire group to see them. By the end of the meeting have them emailed, shared or printed so people leave with real-time minutes.

5. Use structured discussion and problem solving techniques to

enable open and honest discussion and participation by all. We all know it's true: Too often, people in meetings simply don't speak their minds. Sometimes the problem is a leader who doesn't solicit participation. Sometimes a dominant personality intimidates the rest of the group. But most of the time the problem is a simple lack of trust. People don't feel secure enough to say what they really think.

To promote contribution and honesty use thinking and discussion techniques such as Edward de Bono's 6-Thinking Hats[2]. Problem solving

---

[2] Learning Short-take®: 'Creative Business Thinking' provides further information on De Bono's Six Thinking Hats, and other ideas generation and problem solving techniques.

techniques such as flowcharting, Multi-voting, Prioritization Matrix, Brainstorming, Cause & Effect Analysis, and Gantt Charts help to provide structured thinking and encourage attendee involvement. Also, setting a ground rule from the beginning of the meeting that if attendees don't like an idea then they should speak up, may prompt some attendees to speak their minds with more license.

6. Get real data into the meeting rooms.

Meetings are always missing important information, so they postpone critical decisions. The Agenda should clearly state the information that's required for the meeting. People are likely to use the Agenda as a handy checklist prior to attending the meeting.

7. Practice Makes Perfect

Monitor what works and what doesn't and hold people accountable. Meetings are like any other part of business life: you get better only if you commit to it and aim high. Most people don't have good meetings because they don't know what good meetings are like. Good meetings aren't just about work. They're about fun and keeping people charged up. It's more than collaboration, it's about freeing people up to think more creatively."

 **Complete Activity # 4**
Meeting Strategies

ACTIVITY 4: MEETING STRATEGIES

Select your top three strategies for fixing problem meetings and record how you will implement these strategies to improve meeting outcomes in your workplace.

Top Three Meeting Strategies	How I will implement these for improved meeting success
1.	
2.	
3.	

Now update your Learning Journal (page 73)

TYPES OF MEETINGS

Meetings can be classified into two major categories

Information Meetings	Decision-Making Meetings
Advise / Update Sell an idea/concept	Goal Setting Problem Solving

Key differences in types of meetings

	Information	Decision-Making
Number of attendees	Any	Small - preferably 12 or fewer
Who should attend	Those who need to know	Those responsible and those who can contribute
Communication	One-way presentation	Two-way & interactive
In-person Room Set-up	Classroom or theater style	Conference style
Effective style of leadership	Authoritative	Participative
Emphasis should be on…	Content	Interaction and problem-solving
Key to success	Planning and preparation of information to be presented	Meeting climate that supports open, free expression

Complete Activity # 5
What Type of Meeting Am I?

ACTIVITY 5: WHAT TYPE OF MEETING AM I?

Review the statements in the left column below and identify which type of meeting they relate to. Indicate the meeting type by placing an 'IM' for Information Meeting or 'DMM' for Decision Making Meeting in the right column.

Statement	Which type of meeting am I? IM = Information Meeting DMM = Decision Making Meeting
The key to success of this meeting is a climate that supports open, free expression.	
The in-person room set-up should be classroom or theater style.	
Only those responsible and those who can contribute to the discussion should attend.	
The most effective style of leadership for this meeting is authoritative.	
The emphasis of the meeting should be on interaction and problem-solving.	
This type of meeting is about two-way and interactive communication.	
The key to success of this meeting is planning and preparation of information to be presented.	
The purpose of this meeting is goal setting and problem solving.	
Any number of attendees may participate.	
The most effective style of leadership for this meeting is participative.	
The purpose of this meeting is to advise or update, or to sell an idea/concept.	
Only those who need to know should attend.	

Activity # 5 - Check your Answers

Check your work from the previous activity.

Statement	Which type of meeting am I? IM = Information Meeting DMM = Decision Making Meeting
The key to success of this meeting is a climate that supports open, free expression.	**Decision Making Meeting**
The in-person room set-up should be classroom or theater style.	**Information Meeting**
Only those responsible and those who can contribute to the discussion should attend.	**Decision Making Meeting**
The most effective style of leadership for this meeting is authoritative.	**Information Meeting**
The emphasis of the meeting should be on interaction and problem-solving.	**Decision Making Meeting**
This type of meeting is about two-way and interactive communication.	**Decision Making Meeting**
The key to success of this meeting is planning and preparation of information to be presented.	**Information Meeting**
The purpose of this meeting is goal setting and problem solving.	**Decision Making Meeting**
Any number of attendees may participate.	**Information Meeting**
The most effective style of leadership for this meeting is participative.	**Decision Making Meeting**
The purpose of this meeting is to advise or update, or to sell an idea/concept.	**Information Meeting**
Only those who need to know should attend.	**Information Meeting**

Now update your Learning Journal (page 73)

MEETING PURPOSE

Depending in the type of meeting in question, the following suggestions can add real depth to the purpose of a meeting, in addition to the typical "state of the nation" agenda.

1. To train or retrain

Meetings provide an opportunity to train or retrain attendees as appropriate for the objectives of the group. Training should be more practical than theoretical and information must be specific and useful to participants. Attendees should be able to leave the meeting and immediately implement what has been taught. Any ongoing training should be consistent with overall team and business goals.

"Meetings without an agenda are like a restaurant without a menu."

SUSAN B. WILSON

2. To improve communications

Ensure that attendees are informed of any policy changes or changes to business direction which impact on their performance and/or meeting purpose. When there is good or bad news to share, meetings provide an effective forum for communicating information and dispelling the 'rumor mill'…

3. To motivate the team

Participants should always leave a meeting more energized than when they arrived. Use meetings to celebrate successes, provide reward or recognition, and keep the group focussed on achieving team objectives.

4. To solve problems

Meetings can be an effective trouble-shooting forum, for testing the business impact of various decisions. A meeting can be devoted to problem solving so long as the issues are relevant to all attending.

*"The meeting of two personalities is like the contact of two chemical substances:
if there is any reaction, both are transformed."*

CARL JUNG

MEETINGS PROCESS

PART 3

THE MEETING PROCESS

The 3 Step Process for Success!

Step 1 - **Plan the Meeting**

Step 2 - **Prepare the Agenda**

Step 3 - **Conduct the Meeting**

STEP 1 - PLAN THE MEETING

Before you Meet

90% of an effective meeting happens before it takes place. Even the briefest, most informal meeting will benefit from preparation. A formal meeting involving more than a few people must be organized thoroughly.

In a survey of business managers those who say they *always*:

- Define the meeting's purpose   66%
- Address each item on the agenda   62%
- Assign follow-up action   59%
- Take minutes of the meeting   47%
- Invite only essential participants   46%
- Write an agenda with time frames   36%

There is significant room for improvement, to increase meeting effectiveness.

Planning Timetable

Planning for an effective meeting begins 10 days prior to the event. Following is a planning timetable to facilitate meeting success. This is for an In-person meeting. Timings for Virtual meetings may be shorter than those stated.

Task	Day	Action
Notice of Meeting	-10	Chair / Administrator
Participant additions to the agenda and Submission of papers	-7	Participants
Agenda agreed and distributed	-6	Chair / Administrator
Day of meeting	0	All
Minutes distributed	+2	Administrator

Complete Activity # 6
Meeting Planner

Complete Activity # 7
Worksheet for Next 6 Meetings

ACTIVITY 6: MEETING PLANNER

For regular meetings that you organize (i.e. those meetings scheduled on a regular basis well in advance), complete the following to help you plan for success.

1) **How often will you conduct regular/ standing meetings?**	
2) **Location / Start Time / Finish Time**	
3) **Broad Meeting Purpose** - Decision - Discussion - Information - Planning - Generating ideas - Getting feedback - Finding solutions - Agreeing (targets, budgets, aims, etc) - Policy statement - Team-building/ motivation - Guest speaker - information, initiatives, etc	(Highlight areas to discuss at your standing/regular meetings - add notes below for more specific ideas.)

ACTIVITY 6: CONTINUED

4) **Specific Meeting Tracks**
   - To communicate or request vital information.
   - When you need a group consensus.
   - To respond to questions or concerns.
   - When you need a decision or an evaluation on an issue.
   - When you need acceptance or support of an idea.
   - To sell an idea, product or service.
   - To brainstorm ideas.
   - To solve a problem, conflict or difference of opinion.
   - To generate a sense of team spirit.
   - To provide training or clarification of a project.
   - To provide reassurance on an issue or situation.
   - To create an awareness or interest in an idea, situation or project.

(Highlight areas to discuss at standing/regular meetings - add notes below for more specific ideas.)

ACTIVITY 6: CONTINUED

5) **Ideas of what to do in Meetings**
   - Show films and videos.
   - Update product/ processes/corporate/ other knowledge.
   - Use games/activities to increase pace and lift moral. Discuss case histories.
   - Lead role-playing.
   - Feature top performers (have them present back on series of structured questions).
   - Conduct brainstorming sessions.
   - Invite guest speaker.

Match these ideas (and your own) with the plan above and add notes below for more specific details.

Now update your Learning Journal (page 73)

ACTIVITY 7: WORKSHEET FOR NEXT 6 MEETINGS

1. Review the Meeting Planner that you have completed in the previous activity.
2. Consolidate your thoughts and using the table below, create a plan for the next six meetings.

Meeting Date/Time	Main Themes (What)	The Way it will be Conducted (How)
1)		
2)		
3)		
4)		
5)		
6)		

Now update your Learning Journal (page 73)

STEP 2 - PREPARE THE AGENDA

Every meeting should have an agenda and the agenda should be distributed to attendees in advance. Ideally, participants should have an opportunity to contribute to an agenda prior to the meeting.

Whoever controls the agenda controls the meeting. If there is no stated public agenda, the meeting may be taken over by private agendas. The result will be confusion, frustration and failure.

The Agenda

- Communicates important information such as:
    1. Topics for discussion.
    2. Presenter or discussion leader for each topic.
    3. Time allotment for each topic.
- Provides an outline for the meeting (how long to spend on which topics).
- Can be used as a checklist to ensure that all information is covered.
- Lets participants know what will be discussed if it's distributed before the meeting. This gives them an opportunity to come to the meeting prepared for the upcoming discussions or decisions.
- Provides a focus for the meeting (the objective of the meeting must be clearly stated in the agenda).

How to Create an Effective Agenda

1. **Send an e-mail stating the need for a meeting.** The goal of the meeting and administrative details such as when and where the meeting will be held. Ask those invited to accept or decline their attendance. Make it clear that once they have accepted the invitation, they are expected to attend.

2. **Ask participants for input to the agenda.** Request that attendees contact you no less than two days before the meeting with their request for an agenda item, and ask them to estimate the amount of time they will need to present it.

3. **Finalize Agenda.** Once all of the agenda requests have been submitted summarize them in a table format with the Headings Agenda Item, Presenter and Time. It is your responsibility to ensure that each agenda item is directly related to the goals of this particular meeting. If an inappropriate request is made, suggest that person send an e-mail or memo instead or recommend that this agenda item be discussed at another meeting. Also, you need to be realistic about the amount of time you allocate to each presenter.

4. **Distribute the agenda to all the meeting participants the day before the meeting** with a reminder of the meeting goals, location, time and duration. At this time, ask the presenters if they are happy with the order in which they will be speaking and the amount of time they have been allocated.

5. **Follow the Agenda** during the meeting.

Agenda essentials

The agenda should indicate what will happen at the meeting.

Formal Agenda Flow

The most formal of agendas will include, in this order:

- The title of the meeting
- Meeting date, time, venue
- Apologies for absence
- Minutes of the previous meeting
- Matters arising from the previous meeting
- Reports from sub-committees
- Other items to be discussed
- Contributions from guest speakers / consultants
- The date, time, and venue of the next meeting

> **KEEP ENERGY LEVELS UP**
>
> Schedule a break for a meeting that is longer than 1 hour. (15-minute breaks should be taken every 60-90 minutes)

General Agenda Flow

All agendas should include:

- The title of the meeting
- Date, time, venue (including directions and parking as appropriate)
- For virtual meetings provide joining instructions and tech requirements
- Preparation Required
- Other information as necessary, eg for out-of-town participants:
    - Travel arrangements (flights, accommodation, maps)
    - Expense arrangements (travel, accommodation, meals, sundries)

Complete Activity # 8
Meeting Agenda

ACTIVITY 8: MEETING AGENDA

 Download the TPC Meeting Agenda from https://www.catherinematttiske.com/books

 **Activity using the TPC Meeting Agenda**

- Carefully review the tool
- Modify or amend the tool for your organizational needs

Now update your Learning Journal (page 73)

 **Complete Activity # 9**
Meeting Administration Checklist

ACTIVITY 9: MEETING ADMINISTRATION CHECKLIST

 Download the **TPC Meeting Administration Checklist** from https://www.catherinematttiske.com/books

Activity using the TPC Meeting Administration Checklist

- Carefully review the tool
- Modify or amend the tool for your organizational needs

Now update your Learning Journal (page 73)

Tips for Starting your Meeting On-time

If you are the Meeting Organizer:

- **State that the meeting will begin promptly** at the scheduled time and that all participants should be on time.

- **Use your internal meeting scheduler or send a reminder e-mail 30 minutes before** the meeting begins and encourage meeting participants to arrive on time.

- **Ensure that you begin the meeting at the scheduled time.** If you've encouraged others to be prompt, don't embarrass yourself by showing up late.

- **(In-person) Close the meeting room doors at the scheduled time.**

  There's nothing like late attendees to disrupt the flow of a meeting! Consider posting a note outside the door stating the meeting's time. This may seem harsh, but it clearly communicates how serious you are about keeping your meetings on time. If the tardy participants don't consider your meeting important enough to arrive on time, perhaps they shouldn't have committed to attend at all.

- **If your meeting starts a little late, you should still finish the meeting at the scheduled time.** It is inconsiderate to assume the participants' schedules revolve around your meeting, so wrap up the meeting when you promised.

If you are the Attendee:

- **Quickly review the agenda before heading to the meeting.** It's a good idea to remind yourself why you're attending the meeting. Reviewing the agenda helps attendees be better prepared for the meeting and, in turn, will help focus the meeting, enable all of the agenda items to be covered and allow the meeting to finish on time.

- **Make your way to/ open a virtual meeting at least 10 minutes before it actually begins.** This will give you enough time to set up, pour a cup of coffee or deal with any issues that may come up along the way. Plus, you'll get the best seat for the meeting!

- **Consider speaking up if the meeting organizer shows up late.** There are several ways to do this tactfully without insulting anyone. For example, if the organizer consistently arrives 10 minutes late to your weekly meetings, ask them if it would be more convenient to start 15 minutes later next week.

- **Try to ask only relevant questions** during the meeting. If your comment isn't directly related to the topic at hand, don't mention it. Getting off track is one of the main reasons that meetings go over time. If your group can avoid getting off track, you'll all spend less time in meetings.

- **Leave the meeting when it was scheduled to end.** When the organizer extended the invitation to meet, they stated when the meeting would finish. It was on this condition that you accepted the meeting and committed your time. If you have work to which you must attend, politely tell the organizer that you have to leave and excuse yourself from the meeting.

STEP 3 - CONDUCT THE MEETING

Things to include…

1. Take Minutes
2. Create a strong opening
3. Use Visual Aids
4. Encourage discussion by using questions
5. Handle difficult situations

1. Take Minutes

At some point you will be asked to take minutes at a meeting. This task isn't reserved for secretaries only. Since the minutes will serve as an official record of what took place during the meeting, you must be accurate. Here are some pointers to help you master this skill.

Before the Meeting: Prepare to Take Minutes

- Choose your tool: Decide how you will take notes, i.e. pen and paper, laptop computer, audio recorder, shared document, virtual collaboration board.
  - Having a data project connected to, or sharing the screen of the computer on which minutes are taken is an excellent way to ensure that no meeting attendee is oblivious to his or her assigned tasks. This method also reduces the opportunity for mistakes in the minutes.
- Make sure your tool of choice is in working order and have a backup just in case.
- Use the meeting agenda to formulate an outline.
- Obtain a list of meeting attendees and make sure you know 'who's who'.
- Prepare an attendance sheet.

During the Meeting: Take Minutes

- Pass around an attendance sheet. In a virtual meeting take a screenshot of the participant list, or ask everyone to put their name onto a whiteboard.
- Note the time the meeting begins.
- Don't try to write down every single comment, just the main ideas.
- Write down any decisions and who made them.
- Record assigned tasks - be clear when writing the task, who is assigned the task, the due date for completing the task.
- Make note of any follow-up issues for the next meeting.
- Note the ending time of the meeting.
- It using a laptop computer, digital recorder or shared file, you may be able to print, email or share the minutes during the meeting and distribute them immediately.

After the Meeting: Finalize Minutes

- Type up or review and finalize the minutes as soon as possible after the meeting (if not done during the meeting), while everything is still fresh in your mind.
- Include the name of organization, name of committee, type of meeting (daily, weekly, monthly, annual, or special), and purpose of meeting.
- Include the time the meeting began and ended.
- Proof read the minutes before submitting them.

Complete Activity # 10
Meeting Minutes

ACTIVITY 10: MEETING MINUTES

 Download the TPC Meeting Minutes
from https://www.catherinematttiske.com/books

 **Activity using the TPC Meeting Minutes**

- Carefully review the tool
- Modify or amend the tool for your organizational needs

Now update your Learning Journal (page 73)

2. Create a Strong Opening

It is critical in the first few moments of the meeting to engage attendees and connect them with the purpose and objectives of the meeting.

Make a Positive First Impression

First impressions are intuitive behavior, read by the conscious and subconscious mind. You do not have to speak at all... in order to make a first impression. In fact, when you first meet someone, what you say verbally may not be as important as how you appear.

Enhance your ability to make a powerful and positive first impression using body language, eye contact, handshake, poise, posture and the lost art of manners. These are all components of successful business and personal savvy. Your ability to handle yourself with professionalism is part of the new measure of success.

Begin the Meeting on Time

- The person you are meeting with for the first time is not interested in your 'good excuse' for being late. Plan to arrive a few minutes early. Allow flexibility for possible delays, such as traffic, taking a wrong turn, or additional time taken for clearing office security.

- If you are hosting a meeting, your punctuality and ability to begin the meeting on time sends a strong message to the other attendees. By waiting for others to arrive, tells attendees that you'll wait for them at the next meeting. Perhaps wait one or two minutes and get started.

Relax

- If you are nervous about the meeting, try to think of a positive outcome. Showing your nerves will put the other meeting attendees on edge. If you are calm and confident others will feel more at ease and the meeting will flow smoothly.

Look the part

- Physical appearance is the first thing people see when they meet you. You don't have to be a super model, you need to dress and look appropriate.

- Appropriate dress for meetings will depend on where, when and with whom you are meeting. In a business setting, think about what is appropriate and the impression you would like to make.

- Ensure your personal grooming is professional.

- Pay particular attention when traveling to other countries about what the local culture finds acceptable for dress and grooming as their business standard.

"They may forget what you said, but they will never forget how you made them feel."

CARL W. BUECHNER

Smile

- A warm and confident smile will put both yourself and other meeting attendees at ease.

Be Confident

- Body language speaks much louder than words. Project confidence and self assurance by standing tall, smiling, making eye contact, greeting with a firm handshake and listening to others.

Focus

- Ensure that you create an environment where there are no distractions. Close the door of the meeting room, turn off phones, and do anything else to create a distraction free zone.

- Manage the distraction of others. If the meeting room has a window, sit facing the window, so that the other attendees are not facing the window, therefore, they will be less distracted. If someone else's phone rings, stop the meeting and wait for the person to turn it off, answer it, or leave the room. While distractions are happening, the meeting is focused on the distraction, not on what you are saying.

Be Interested and Interesting

- Think about questions that you can ask other meeting attendees. These can be personal questions used as small talk while waiting for the meeting to begin, or business questions to be used before, during or after the meeting.
- Take a few minutes to learn something about each person at the meeting. This is especially effective for people you are to meet with for the first time.
- Think of likely questions that you might be asked - both personally and professionally. Think of interesting answers which will help create the impression that you want to project.

Half a glass full

- Attitude shows in everything we do. In difficult situations in a meeting, focus on the positive rather than the negative. Even in the face of criticism or nervousness take a moment to reframe your attitude to being positive, maintaining an upbeat manner and a smile.

"Euphemisms are unpleasant truths wearing diplomatic cologne."

QUENTIN CRISP

"Divide and rule, a sound motto. Unite and lead, a better one."

JOHANN WOLFGANG VON GOETHE

Take Control

State your message. Inform the attendees how long you will speak for, what you expect of them, and how various discussion items will be handled.

Set Meeting Ground Rules

Establishing ground rules and gaining consensus from the group that they will all adhere to the rules, is a good way to circumvent problems down the track. Examples of ground rules include:

1. Starting the meeting on-time.
2. The agenda will be followed.
3. Decisions will be made by consensus.
4. Opinions are encouraged.
5. Listen and respect all attendees.

Alternatively an activity can be set at the beginning of meetings to draw out appropriate meeting behavior. Using a flipchart or whiteboard the Meeting Organizer asks the group to brainstorm 'Distracting Behavior' and 'Contributing Behavior'. Attendees are more likely to be consistent with the Contributing Behavior as a result of undertaking such an activity. In the words of Bob Pike "People believe their own data!"

Acknowledge meeting attendees

Why is the meeting relevant to them? How will it benefit them?

Establish your credentials

What experience do you have? What have you done as background for the meeting?

Introduce the subject matter

Explain the purpose of your presentation and the structure that you will follow. Name the main categories. Remember the primary effect and make sure this introduction is so noteworthy that it will be long remembered along with its messages. The audience will now be confident that you know what you are doing. This will allow them to relax and actually listen to you!

Note - For more information on Presentation Skills you may like to complete the Learning Short-take® - Persuasive Presentation Skills.

3. Use Visual Aids

Pictures can convey what can't be conveyed by words alone.

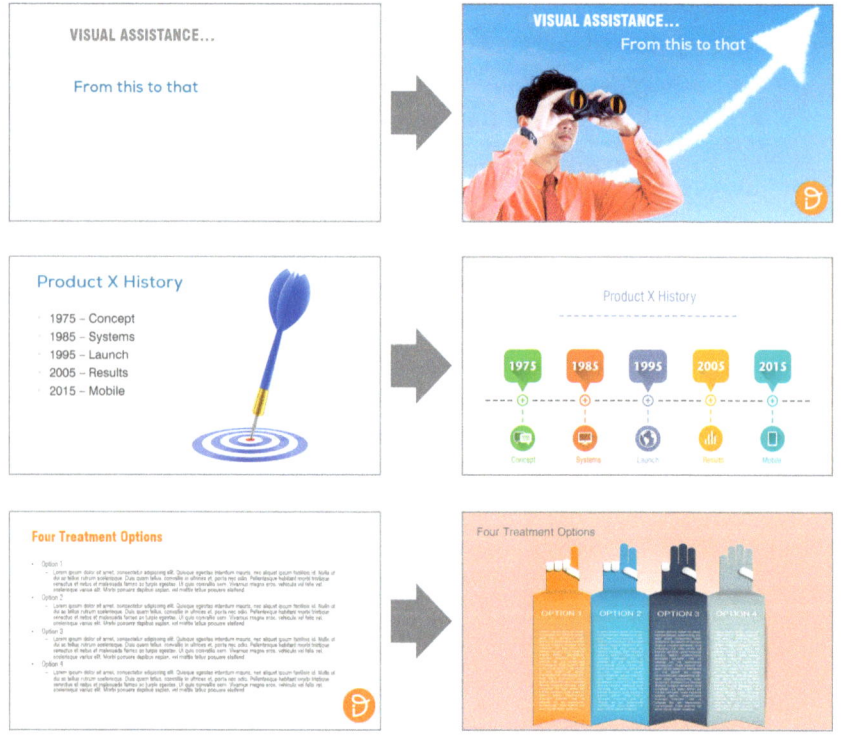

4. Encourage Discussion by using Questions

#1 - Asking for feelings and opinions

Use a method of asking questions that will help people express their ideas, draw people out, and encourage discussion. For example:

- What is your reaction to…?
- How do you feel about…?
- What is your thinking on…?
- What brings you to conclude that…?
- What are some other ways to get at…?

#2 - Paraphrase

One way to help people reach mutual understanding is to paraphrase, that is, to ask one person to repeat what someone else said and to state what that person meant:

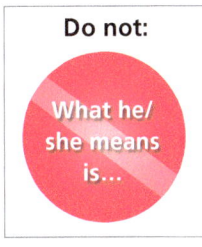

- Are you asking me to…?
- Let me see if I understand your position. Are you saying that…?
- Before we go on, let me paraphrase what I think you are proposing…
- Let me restate you last point to see if I understand.
- Before you go on, do you mean that…?

#3 - Encourage Participation

Sometimes people tend to hold back. They can be encouraged to participate by such questions as:

- Lee, how do you feel about this?
- Austin, how would you answer Sam's question?
- Before we go on, I would like to hear from Brook on this.
- We have heard from everyone but Jane. Jane, what is your feeling on this?
- We haven't heard from Jack yet. Jack, what is your opinion here?

#4 - Ask for a Summary

- Many good ideas have been presented in the last few minutes. Will someone please summarize the major points before we go on?
- I have heard a number of proposals. Bill, will you summarize what has been agreed upon?
- It is clear Jim does not agree. Jim, will you summarize your major objections?
- I have lost track. Let's summarize what has been done so far.

#5 - Ask for Clarification

- I didn't understand your last comment. What would you do if…?
- The examples you gave concern week day operations - do they also affect weekends?
- I saw Kate shaking her head. Kate would it help if we took a minute to explain the history?

#6 - Explore an idea in more detail

- What are some other ways to approach this problem?
- Are there other things we should consider?
- Tan, what would you add to what has been said?

#7 - Be Supporting

- Let's give Tony a chance to tell it the way he sees it.
- Dave, you have had your say. Now it's Jodie's turn. Give her a chance to explain.
- That's a good point, thanks Heather.

#8 - Question Assumptions

- Your proposal assumes that unless we use threats, they won't cooperate. Is that right?
- Your suggestion assumes that we can't meet the schedule. Is that correct?
- Your objection assumes that we will not get promised deliveries. Is that a good assumption?
- We mustn't make decisions on their behalf. Let's survey their opinions and discuss the results next meeting.

Now update your Learning Journal (page 73)

5. Handle Difficult Situations

"Did you ever notice how difficult it is to argue with someone who is not obsessed with being right?"

WAYNE DYER

1. **Clarify Objectives** - restate the purpose of the meeting and bring the discussion back to the 'issues' not the 'emotions'.

2. **Strive for Understanding** - use effective questioning to really understand the other person's point of view. Open questions invite detailed responses and provide others with an opportunity to express their concerns and 'let off some steam'. Paraphrase to ensure you have understood what they have said. Again focus on the facts and not the people involved.

3. **Focus on the Rational** - as above, focus on the issues that are important, not the people and the emotions involved. 'Issues' tend to be rational, 'people' have a tendency to be irrational.

4. **Generate Alternatives** - problem solve the issues by generating a number of possible solutions, then ranking solutions according to relevant parameters ie. cost, time, quality, impact on people etc.

5. **Table the Issue** - if the issue cannot be resolved within the scope of the current meeting, 'parking lot' the item and return to it after the meeting or at a later meeting. In either case, ensure there is appropriate follow-up and that meeting attendees are advised of progress on the issue.

6. **Use Humour** - where possible, inject some humor into the issue. This will help to diffuse emotions and bring the focus back to the task at hand.

"In the middle of every difficulty lies opportunity."

ALBERT EINSTEIN

Complete Activity # 11
Handling Difficult Meeting Situations

ACTIVITY 11: HANDLING DIFFICULT MEETING SITUATIONS

Select the most appropriate response to each of the questions below. Read all answers and rank in order of your likely response - e.g. A C B D

1) **You arrive early and find the meeting room is arranged differently than you would like although you feel you could get by with the present arrangement.**
   a) Call the group responsible for the room and have it rearranged
   b) Rearrange the room yourself
   c) Wait until participants begin to arrive and have someone help rearrange things
   d) Leave the room as is, and complain later to the group responsible.

   Ranked Response _____

2) **You expect 10 participants at a 9:00am meeting. It is 9:05 and only eight have arrived. No one advised you of plans to arrive late.**
   a) Begin the meeting with those present
   b) Telephone the two participants to see if they are coming
   c) Wait another five minutes and then begin
   d) Ask those present to vote on whether to begin now or later

   Ranked Response _____

3) **Some participants are not contributing to the meeting although they appear to be attentive.**
   a) Monitor the situation and see if it continues
   b) Ask a non-contributing participant for an opinion or reaction
   c) Ask a non-contributing participant why they are not involved
   d) Do nothing – they'll speak up if they want to.

   Ranked Response _____

4) **You want discussion on a topic but no one is talking.**
   a) Ask a general question of the group
   b) Ask a specific question of an individual
   c) Ask for feedback on why no one's talking
   d) Adjourn the meeting due to lack of interest.

   Ranked Response _____

ACTIVITY 11: CONTINUED

5) You notice, through nonverbal clues that the interest level of the group is fading.
   a) Shorten your agenda and adjourn the meeting
   b) Take a five-minute break
   c) Speak more loudly and in a more animated fashion
   d) Try to start discussion.

   Ranked Response _____

6) The group is getting away from the objective of the meeting:
   a) Let things go as long as everyone seems interested
   b) Interrupt and bring the group back to the agenda
   c) Interrupt and vote on whether or not to continue this discussion
   d) Take a break so participants can continue the discussion on their own time and reconvene when it is over.

   Ranked Response _____

7) It is time for the posted break. When you announce the break your boss, who is a participant in the meeting, says it isn't necessary.
   a) Confront your boss on who's running the meeting
   b) Cancel the break and continue with the meeting
   c) Take a break and let your boss continue the meeting
   d) Ask the group if it wants to take a break.

   Ranked Response _____

Activity # 11 - Check your Answers

Check your work from the previous activity.

> **Quick 7 - Multiple choice**
> **Suggested answers**
>
> 1. ACBD
> 2. ACBD
> 3. ABCD
> 4. ABCD
> 5. CDBA
> 6. BCAD
> 7. DBCA

Now update your Learning Journal (page 73)

BRINGING MEETINGS TO LIFE

PART 4

MAKING MEETINGS MORE LIVELY

When the average employee is asked to attend another meeting during their busy day, their natural response is often negative. But injecting a little enjoyment into your meetings might be just the thing to encourage participation and creativity. A little laughter can go a long way towards improving productivity and the moral of meeting attendees.

Unless the meeting is scheduled to deliver bad news, some of the following ideas may assist. Many of these ideas work for virtual meetings too.

- **Include Activities.** Most people learn by doing. Whenever possible, include hands-on activities, live demonstrations, field trips, games, role-playing, etc. Don't be afraid to mix it up - variety is what keeps people interested.

- **Enticement works!** Organize contests to generate ideas and offer prizes to encourage participation. A little friendly competition can bring great results.

- **Spend a Penny.** If your meetings tend to be dominated by a few people, try passing out five pennies to each meeting attendee. Attendees must "spend" a penny each time they talk. And no borrowing allowed!

- Consider appointing a **Director of Fun** for meetings. The Director will be responsible for inventing participatory activities, bringing in additional fun materials (videos, comic strips, articles, snacks) that relate to the meeting topic. A different Director could be appointed for each meeting.

- For a fun change of pace, consider **hosting a meeting in talk-show style.** Have the speakers act as guests, attendees are audience members and the meeting facilitator can be the talk show host. The host will encourage the audience to ask questions and share their opinions on the speakers' comments.

- **Contests or quizzes** are other methods of getting your group excited about its meetings. If your meeting objective is to introduce new information, let them know there will be a quiz on the content you're going to present. At the end of your presentation, ask the group questions about the content you've just presented. Whoever provides the correct answer first, receives a prize. Not only will this generate some excitement, but you can guarantee that fewer people will be daydreaming during your presentation!

Energy - Definition:

Strength of expression; force of utterance; power to impress the mind and arouse the feelings; life; spirit; - said of speech, language, words, style; as, a style full of energy.

"In every meeting think about what can you do that makes people think, 'Wow'?"

BARRY WOLPA,
VP GENWORTH FINANCIAL

- **Food** is another useful device for generating excitement in your meetings. Before your meeting, tape, for example, individually-wrapped chocolates under the participants' chairs. After welcoming people to the meeting, tell the group they have "surprises" under their chairs. Everyone enjoys surprises, no matter how small! Not only is this a nice way of saying "welcome" to the meeting, but it's also an inexpensive way to create a fun and exciting tone for the meeting ahead.

- For a small dose of humor, **show a comic strip related to each agenda item** or topic you introduce. Dilbert is great for poking fun at meetings and other aspects of corporate life. If comic strips aren't an option, **share humorous quotes** from famous people during your meetings. The Internet has a plethora of sites dedicated to famous quotes, so finding something that relates directly to your agenda topic will be quick and easy.

- Put a **5-minute time limit on individual topics.** Once the discussion goes over, move on. If the topic warrants further discussion, assign someone the task of scheduling a separate meeting.

- For **one-on-one discussions or updates,** consider taking a walk instead of meeting in the office. If you're both away from the distractions of coworkers, phones and e-mail, you're more likely to concentrate on the issue at hand. If you've scheduled a half-hour meeting, walk for 15 minutes and then turn around. The fresh air will revive you both and the change of scenery just might get your creative juices flowing. If you think you may forget important points, take a tape recorder along and record your conversation.

Having fun at the office leads to a more enjoyable workplace and increased employee loyalty (this is especially important when you're attending the sixth meeting of the day).

"The most successful meetings get that wow-factor through combining approach, location and creativity in a way that bolsters the ultimate business aim"

BRENDAN COFFEY,
EXECUTIVE TRAVEL, MARCH 2006

INTERNATIONAL MEETING ETIQUETTE

According to an old Japanese saying, "the protruding nail gets hammered down." If you've ever committed a major faux pas in an international business meeting, you'll appreciate this statement! In today's increasingly global business environment, it pays to be aware of the international rules of etiquette. When you enter into a relationship with a colleague or client from a different country you should conduct extensive research around foreign operating standards, economic conditions, political environment, etc. Of course it's important to focus on business aspects, but it's just as important to know when and how to hand out business cards, when to accept a gift, and what to order at dinner. The following tips will hopefully save you from some embarrassing moments!

Habits from Home

One of the trickiest things about working with foreign counterparts is the risk that small, everyday gestures could be wildly misinterpreted. For example, nodding your head up and down in North America signifies your agreement with a person. But in Bulgaria, the same action would tell the person you're meeting with that you're disagreeing with them! Physical gestures play an important role when meeting in a foreign country.

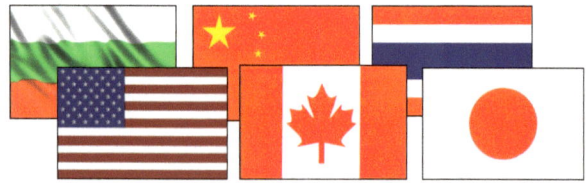

Cultural Conventions

What to wear, which title to use, how to negotiate and whether or not to bring a gift are just some of the quandaries business travelers face. For example, Thailand, it's customary to exchange gifts during your second business meeting. In China, however, gift giving is considered a form of bribery and is actually illegal!

In North America, it's common to call business colleagues by their first names, but this would be inappropriate in Japan. Japanese acquaintances should always be addressed by their title or by their last name with the suffix san. However, the suffix san should not be used for a child, spouse or an absent colleague.

Visiting a foreign culture can be bewildering for even the most intrepid business traveller or global worker. Check on the internet for doing business in your destination country and you'll receive an overview of cultural do's and taboos, appropriate corporate etiquette and handy hints on conducting business in specific areas of the world.

Virtual Venues

Virtual meetings conducted via videoconference or virtual meeting software (or even in the metaverse!), still need to reflect the customs and traditions of the individuals you're meeting with so many of the same rules apply. Virtual meetings also have the added complexity of not physically being with the people you're meeting. A misinterpreted sentence could lead to a major misunderstanding with no chance for rebuttal.

The safest practice when working with others outside of your home country is to do your best to "act local". Then, you can be confident that your overseas meetings will be successful and yours hosts will appreciate your cultural sensitivity and will.

"*Wisdom is the reward you get for a lifetime of listening when you'd have preferred to talk.*"

DOUG LARSON

IN SUMMARY - MAKING MEETINGS WORK

"Asking the right questions takes as much skill as giving the right answers."

ROBERT HALF

Checklist for Conducting Effective Meetings

- ☐ Change the meeting focus from 'down time' to 'work time'.
- ☐ Plan the meeting using the TPC Meeting Planner.
- ☐ Establish and keep to the meeting objective.
- ☐ Prepare and distribute an Agenda prior to the meeting.
- ☐ Gain group consensus on ground rules and meeting etiquette.
- ☐ Keep to the agenda.
- ☐ Record the meeting via Meeting Minutes.
- ☐ Examine interactions whenever emotions or discussion gets heated or fragmented. Ensure the meeting stays on track by revisiting the objectives and Agenda.
- ☐ Create liveliness and interaction in meetings.
- ☐ Be sensitive to cultural issues of attendees.
- ☐ Set tasks as Action Items and insist that meeting attendees take responsibility for the actions.
- ☐ Evaluate each meeting to check your progress on meeting improvement.

Section 2

LEARNING JOURNAL

The Learning Journal is used throughout the process to record your key learnings, hot tips and things to remember.

Update your Learning Journal at anytime. Ensure you complete your Learning Journal after you finish each activity. Then turn back to the Learning Short-take® to continue your learning.

As you work through this Learning Short-take®, make detailed notes on this page of the lessons you have learned and any useful skill areas. For each lesson or refresher point think about how you could further develop this skill. Your coach will want to discuss these with you in your Skill Development Action Planning meeting.

> "…that is what learning is.
> You suddenly understand something you've understood all your life, but in a new way."
>
> DORIS LESSING

> "Act as though it were impossible to fail."
>
> WINSTON CHURCHILL

"The wise do at once what the fool does later."
BALTASAR GRACIAN (1601-58), SPANISH JESUIT PRIEST AND AUTHOR.

Learning or Idea	Action to be taken	Result Expected

Learning Journal - continued

Learning or Idea	Action to be taken	Result Expected

> *"Anyone who stops learning is old, whether at twenty or eighty."*
> HENRY FORD

Learning or Idea	Action to be taken	Result Expected

Learning Journal - continued

"Courage is what it takes to stand up and speak; courage is also what it takes to sit down and listen."

WINSTON CHURCHILL

Section 3

SKILL DEVELOPMENT ACTION PLAN

Your Skill Development Action Plan is the last Step in the process. After you have completed the Learning Short-take® and all Activities, update your Learning Journal, then complete this section.

SKILL DEVELOPMENT ACTION PLAN

This is the most important part of the program - your individual Skill Development Action Plan.

You need to complete this plan before meeting with your manager or prior to on-going coaching. You will discuss it in detail with your manager or coach as he or she will ensure that you have everything you need to complete the tasks and activities.

Once you have completed your **Skill Development Action Plan** schedule a meeting time with your manager or coach to review your plan. Take your Learning Short-take® and all other documentation received during the training course to this meeting.

Remember - you have committed to your **Skill Development Action Plan**, and need to make time to complete your tasks!

"The mind, once stretched by a new idea, never regains its original dimensions."

OLIVER WENDELL HOLMES

"Whatever you can do or dream you can - begin it. Boldness has genius, power and magic."

JOHANN WOLFGANG VON GOETHE

"Imagination is the eye of the soul."
JOSEPH JOUBERT (1754-1824)

Task or activity (Be specific)	Measure (this will help you to know you have achieved it)	Date (Be specific)
Reflect on your Learning Journal. Transfer action items that you can apply to your job. Ensure that you include some 'stretch goals' and also a blend of short, medium and long term goals.	Apart from you, who else is needed to assist you in achieving your goal.	Be specific. A general date such as 'Quarter 1', 'August', or 'by end of year' is vague and more likely to result in not achieving your target. Be specific – e.g. 22nd November.

Ideas

CONGRATULATIONS!

You've now completed this Learning Short-take®.

Meet with your Manager/Coach to discuss your
Skill Development Action Plan.

Suggested Reading

1. Streibel, Barbara, 2002. The Managers Guide to Effective Meetings. McGraw-Hill.

2. Doyle, M, and Straus, S, 1986. How to Make Meetings Work. Jove.

3. Lencioni, Patrick, 2004. Death by Meeting: A Leadership Fable... About Solving the most Painful Problem in the Business. Jossey-Bass.

4. Catherine Mattiske, 2020. Leading Virtual Teams: Managing from a Distance During the Coronavirus.

QUICK REFERENCE

This Quick Reference provides you with a summary of key concepts, models and reference material from Learning Short-takes®. We have also included some quotations to ponder.

Use this section as a quick reference to keep your learning active.

Quick Reference

Meeting Traps

1. The meeting is unnecessary.
2. The meeting is held for the wrong reason.
3. The objective of the meeting is unclear.
4. The wrong people are present.
5. The agenda is not properly controlled.
6. It takes place in a disagreeable environment.
7. The meeting is poorly timed.
8. The process is subject to poor decision making.

12 Reasons People Need to Meet

1. To communicate or request vital information.
2. When you need a group consensus.
3. To respond to questions or concerns.
4. When you need a decision or an evaluation on an issue.
5. When you need acceptance or support of an idea.
6. To sell an idea, product or service.
7. To brainstorm ideas.
8. To solve a problem, conflict or difference of opinion.
9. To generate a sense of team spirit.
10. To provide training or clarification of a project.
11. To provide reassurance on an issue or situation.
12. To create an awareness or interest in an idea, situation or project.

Quick Reference

Types of Meetings

Information Meetings	Decision-Making Meetings
Advise / Update Sell an idea/concept	Goal Setting Problem solving

Key differences in types of meetings

	Information	Decision-Making
Number of attendees	Any	Small – preferably 12 or fewer
Who should attend	Those who need to know	Those responsible and those who can contribute
Communication	One-way presentation	Two-way & interactive
In-person Room Set-up	Classroom or theater style	Conference style
Effective style of leadership	Authoritative	Participative
Emphasis should be on…	Content	Interaction and problem-solving
Key to success	Planning and preparation of information to be presented	Meeting climate that supports open, free expression

Meeting Planning Timetable

Suggested timing for an In-person meeting. Timings for Virtual meetings may be shorter than those stated.

Task	Day	Action
Notice of Meeting	-10	Chair / Administrator
Participant additions to the agenda and Submission of papers	-7	Participants
Agenda agreed and distributed	-6	Chair / Administrator
Day of meeting	0	All
Minutes distributed	+2	Administrator

Quick Reference

The Agenda

1. Topics for discussion.
2. Presenter or discussion leader for each topic.
3. Time allotment for each topic.

General Agenda Flow

- The title of the meeting.
- Date, time, venue (including directions and parking as appropriate).
- For virtual meetings provide joining instructions and tech requirements
- Preparation required.
- Proper attire (as appropriate).
- Meal arrangements (as appropriate).
- Other information for out-of-town participants.
  - Travel arrangements (flights, accommodation, maps).
  - Expense arrangements (travel, accommodation, meals, sundries).

Quick Reference

Tips for Starting Your Meeting On-Time

If you're the Meeting Organizer:

- State that the meeting will begin promptly.
- Use your internal meeting scheduler or send a reminder e-mail 30 minutes before.
- Ensure that you begin the meeting at the scheduled time.
- Close the meeting room doors at the scheduled time.
- If your meeting starts a little late, you should still finish the meeting at the scheduled time.

If you're the Attendee:

- Quickly review the agenda before heading to the meeting.
- Make your way to the meeting 10 minutes before it actually begins.
- Consider speaking up if the meeting organizer shows up late.
- Try to ask only relevant questions during the meeting.
- Leave the meeting when it was scheduled to end.

Conduct the Meeting

- Take Minutes.
- Create a strong opening.
- Use Visual Aids.
- Encourage discussion by using questions.
- Handle difficult situations.
- Handle conflict

Quick Reference

Encouraging Meeting Discussion

1. Asking for feelings and opinions.
2. Paraphrase.
3. Encourage participation.
4. Ask for a summary.
5. Ask for clarification.
6. Explore an idea in more detail.
7. Be supporting.
8. Question assumptions.

Handling Meeting Conflict

1. Clarify Objectives.
2. Strive for Understanding.
3. Focus on the Rational.
4. Generate Alternatives.
5. Table the Issue.
6. Use Humour.

"*The trouble with talking too fast is you may say something you haven't thought of yet.*"

ANN LANDERS

NEXT STEPS

Congratulations! You have now completed this Learning Short-take® title. The entire list of Learning Short-takes® can be found on the catherinemattiske.com website.

In this section we have suggested Learning Short-take® titles for you that will build your learning. You may order these Learning Short-takes® online at https://www.catherinemattiske.com/books or from your bookstores.

Persuasive Presentation Skills
Create, Prepare and Design with Confidence

Learning Short-take® Outline

Persuasive Presentation Skills combines self-study with realistic workplace activities to provide presenters with the key skills and techniques to prepare and deliver dynamic presentations. After assessing your current approach to preparing and delivering presentations, **Persuasive Presentation Skills** will help you develop unique and innovative strategies to improve your presentation success from small meetings to large audiences. You will learn to effectively plan your communication by using a real-life upcoming presentation.

A dynamic and powerful presentation gives you a platform to communicate your message effectively, influence your audience and spark desired action. Effective presenters spend a considerable amount of time preparing for their presentation, ensuring that the structure, content and communication style is appropriate for their audience. It is often what happens before the presenter gives their presentation that dictates the success of the presentation.

Persuasive Presentation Skills includes the **Persuasive Presentation Skills Presentation Planner**, provided as a free downloadable tool.

Learning Objectives
- Define the importance of preparation in delivering a successful presentation.
- Know how to structure your presentation to deliver key messages.
- Recognize how to connect with your audience and maintain attention.
- Identify key factors for enhancing your message and projecting credibility.
- Design and use visual aids to support your message.
- Describe how to control your nervous energy.
- Create a Skill Development Action Plan.

Course Content
- Part 1: Creating Effective Presentations
  - Overview for Success
- Part 2: Planning Your Presentation
  - 7 Steps for Success
- Part 3: The Presentation Day
  - Reducing Nervousness
  - Tips & Tricks
  - After the Presentation

In Closing...

Confident Facilitation Skills
Tools and Techniques for the Professional Facilitator

Course Content

- Part 1: The Role of the Facilitator
- Part 2: Preparing for Facilitation
- Part 3: Conducting the Session
- Part 4: Dealing with Difficult Situations
- Part 5: Problem Solving Techniques

Learning Short-take® Outline

Confident Facilitation Skills combines self-study with realistic workplace activities to provide you with the key skills and techniques to become a more effective facilitator. You will be guided through a comprehensive approach to prepare for a facilitation session, focus the group, draw out ideas, manage difficult behavior, build consensus, maintain high energy, close the session, and construct customized agendas. **Confident Facilitation Skills** also includes a comprehensive reference guide of proven group facilitation techniques.

Facilitation is fast becoming a key skill for anyone who is in a team, leading a project team, heading up a working group, or managing a department. Facilitation is the skill and art of guiding others to solve problems to achieve objectives without personally giving advice or offering solutions. A facilitator provides the structure and process - enabling groups to function effectively and make high-quality decisions.

Confident Facilitation Skills includes the **Confident Facilitation Initial Meeting Planning Tool**, provided to you as a free download.

Learning Objectives

- Define the role of a facilitator.
- Identify the key facilitation principles.
- Describe best practices related to each facilitation principle.
- Differentiate between process and content facilitation.
- Identify the core practices and skills required for effective facilitation.
- Explain how to stimulate group participation and positively handle conflict.
- Create a Skill Development Action Plan.

Influencing for Opportunity
Identify and Maximize Ways to Influence

Course Content

- Part 1: Fundamentals of Influence
- Part 2: Influence: A Choice
- Part 3: Naturally Occurring Influence Patterns
- Part 4: Methods of Persuasion
- Part 5: The Challenges of Influence
- Part 6: Building a life of Influence

Learning Short-take® Outline

Influencing for Opportunity combines self-study with realistic workplace activities to provide you with the key skills and techniques to influence those around you. You will learn the theory of influence, influence principles and strategies, as well as how to plan and prepare for important opportunities to influence. As a result, you should achieve greater results in your organization, work more productively and effectively in a team environment, and develop stronger working relationships with co-workers, suppliers and customers.

The ability to influence others is critical in today's competitive business environment. Being highly skilled in influence enables you to build the relationships you need to get results inside or outside the organization. Employees and managers alike cannot assume they have power over others - they must earn it through influence. Being an influential person is a skill that can be learned and practiced. **Influencing for Opportunity** will help you succeed in the modern corporate environment by increasing your ability to influence others.

Influencing for Opportunity includes a **toolkit of job aids and learning support tools** provided to you as free downloads.

Learning Objectives

- Identify patterns of influence.
- Evaluate how you currently use influence behaviors and identify areas for development.
- Develop influence behaviors for greater personal and business success.
- Establish clear and powerful influence goals.
- Increase influence to overcome resistance.
- Describe how to ask for and receive support.
- Design an approach for formal and informal influence situations; apply the approach to a real-life situation.
- Create a Skill Development Action Plan.

www.catherinemattiske.com